DIWALI

er

BookLife
PUBLISHING

©This edition published in 2023. First published in 2023. BookLife Publishing Ltd. King's Lynn, Norfolk, PE30 4LS, UK

All rights reserved. Printed in China.

A catalogue record for this book is available from the British Library.

HB ISBN: 978-1-83927-469-5
PB ISBN: 978-1-80505-363-7

Written by:
Madeline Tyler

Edited by:
John Wood

Designed by:
Drue Rintoul

All facts, statistics, web addresses and URLs in this book were verified as valid and accurate at time of writing. No responsibility for any changes to external websites or references can be accepted by either the author or publisher.

FSC
www.fsc.org
MIX
Paper from responsible sources
FSC® C113515

CONTENTS

Words that look like this can be found in the glossary on page 24.

CELEBRATE DIWALI WITH ME!

Shubh Diwali! That means 'Happy Diwali' in my language, Hindi. My name is Baiju. I'm here to tell you about Diwali.

Diwali is a big festival that we love celebrating in our <u>community</u>. It's very bright, colourful and happy. Come and celebrate with me!

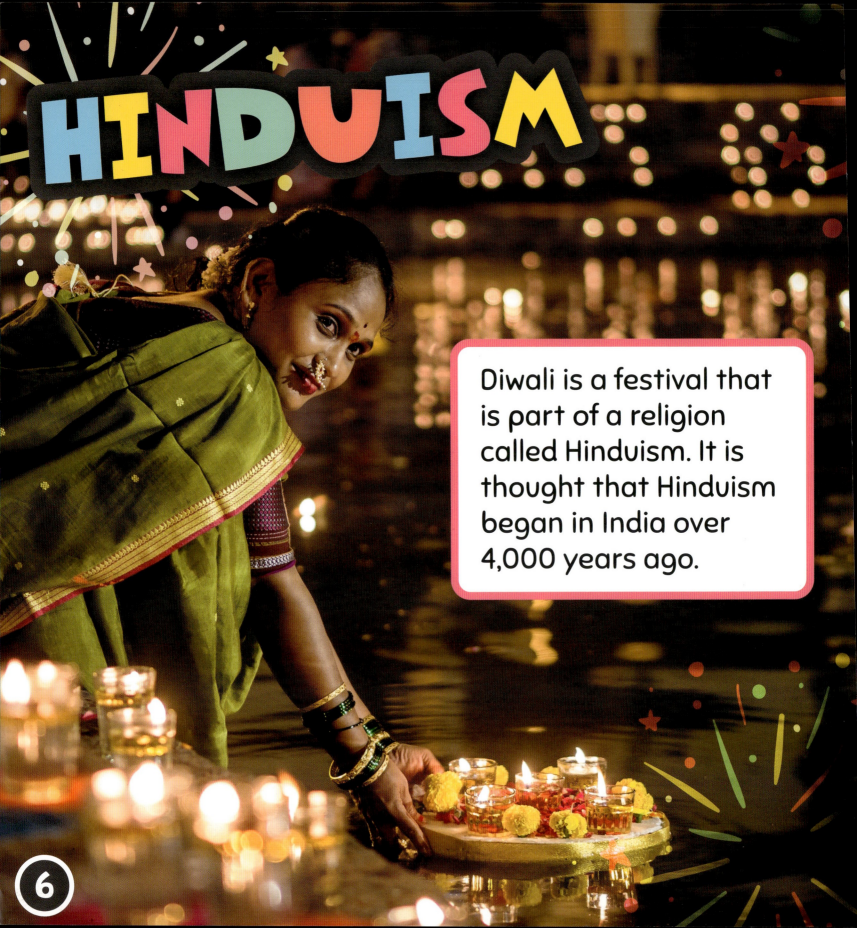

HINDUISM

Diwali is a festival that is part of a religion called Hinduism. It is thought that Hinduism began in India over 4,000 years ago.

We believe in many gods and goddesses. Lord Ganesh is the god of new beginnings and <u>wisdom</u>, and we pray to him at the beginning of things. Lakshmi is the goddess of <u>wealth</u> and good <u>fortune</u>.

Ganesh

Lakshmi

7

DIWALI

Diwali is the festival of lights. We celebrate Diwali some time between October and November.

The word Diwali means 'row of lights'.

Diwali is celebrated by Hindus, **Sikhs** and **Jains**.

Diwali is when we celebrate the Hindu New Year. The festival can last for five days, and it is a fun time to spend with family and friends.

THE STORY OF DIWALI

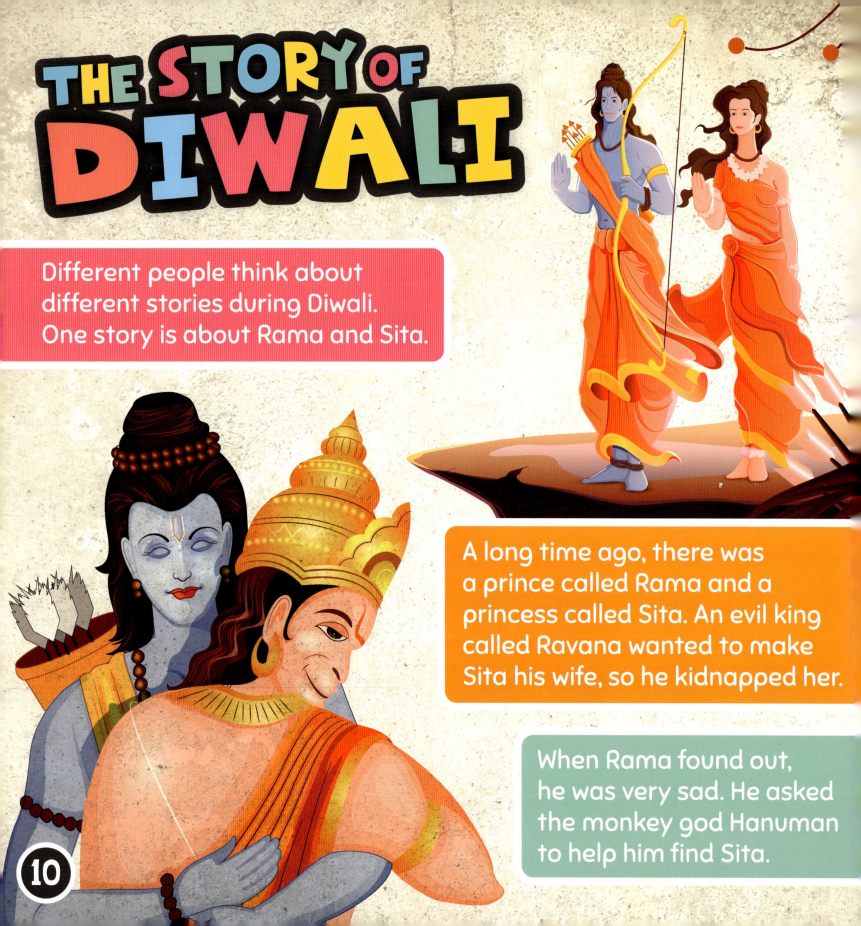

Different people think about different stories during Diwali. One story is about Rama and Sita.

A long time ago, there was a prince called Rama and a princess called Sita. An evil king called Ravana wanted to make Sita his wife, so he kidnapped her.

When Rama found out, he was very sad. He asked the monkey god Hanuman to help him find Sita.

Hanuman found Sita <u>imprisoned</u> on an island. He got his monkey army ready to fight Ravana and free Sita.

It was a big battle and lasted for a long time. Finally, Rama shot Ravana with a magical golden arrow that hit him in the chest. Sita was saved!

It was time for Rama and Sita to go back home, but it was very dark. The villagers lit lamps to help them find their way back.

This is why we light lamps during Diwali!

DIYAS

Diyas are the lamps we light on Diwali. They are very important because they remind some of us of the story of Rama and Sita.

Diyas

Diwali is a time to celebrate good **triumphing** over evil.

Diwali is when we <u>honour</u> Lakshmi. The lights and lamps help Lakshmi to find her way to people's homes and bring them good fortune in the new year.

We also celebrate with sparklers and fireworks.

CLEANING

It is very important for us to have clean homes during Diwali. We clean, tidy and redecorate so that our homes are ready for when Lakshmi visits.

Before Diwali, we go shopping for new clothes. This is so that we can wear new clothes on each day of Diwali. Girls can wear lehengas and boys can wear kurtas.

Kurta

Lehenga

RANGOLI

Rangoli are beautiful patterns made from colourful chalk, rice powder and pastes. Some rangoli patterns are as small as a doorstep, but others are much bigger.

We draw rangoli on the floor outside our homes to welcome guests, including Lakshmi, and bring good luck.

Rangoli patterns can sometimes look like flowers.

PRAYERS AND OFFERINGS

It is common to <u>worship</u> Lord Ganesh and the goddess Lakshmi during Diwali. Many Hindus visit mandirs to pray to them and leave them offerings.

Mandirs are Hindu temples. They are sometimes lit up for Diwali.

At the mandir, we make offerings to Ganesh and Lakshmi. These might be flowers, lit diyas, sweets and other types of food.

The offerings are usually given on a special plate. This is called puja thali.

FESTIVE FOOD

During Diwali, we eat lots of delicious food. We eat lots of sweet foods such as Indian sweets, called mithai. My favourite type is barfi!

Barfi

We offer mithai to the gods, but we also like to give our friends and family boxes of mithai during Diwali.

Mithai

DIWALI AROUND THE WORLD

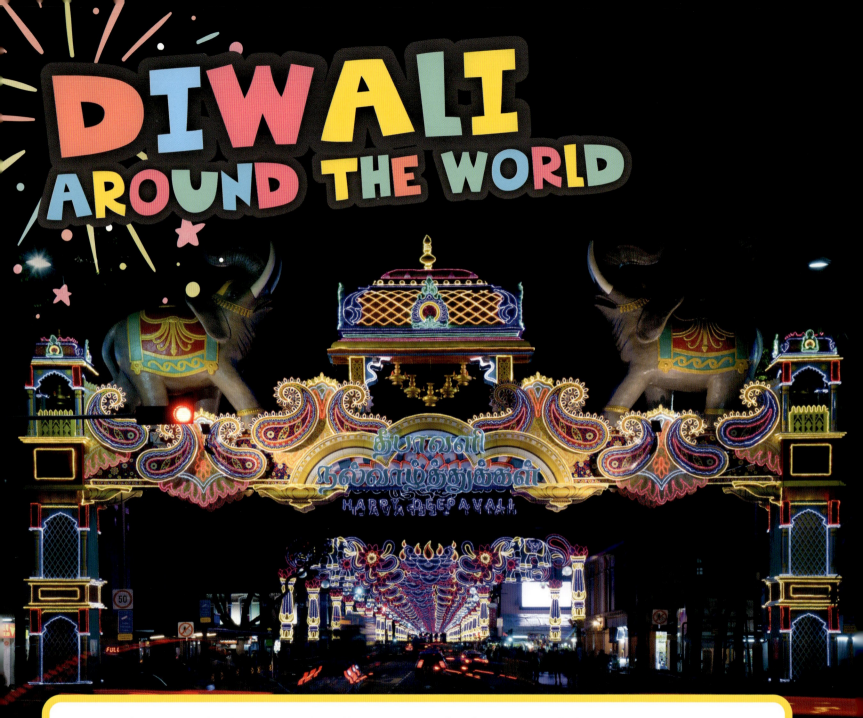

Diwali is celebrated all around the world. In Singapore, there are bright lights and beautiful decorations to celebrate the festival. There are statues of elephants and peacocks, too!

I hope you have learnt a lot about Diwali! If you would like to celebrate Diwali, see whether there are any celebrations happening where you live!

GLOSSARY

community	a group of people who are connected by something
fortune	luck
honour	when lots of people have respect for a person or god and their actions
imprisoned	locked up or held somewhere as a prisoner
Jains	believers in Jainism, a very old Indian religion whose followers do not believe in any gods
Sikhs	members of Sikhism, a religion founded around 500 years ago in South Asia whose followers believe in one God
triumphing	winning in a great victory or success
wealth	a large amount of something, usually money
wisdom	good knowledge, judgement or understanding of something
worship	a religious act where a person shows their love for a god

INDEX